SO-BOG-146

Deterring Criminals
Policy Making and the
American Political Tradition

364.973
Se2d

114834

DATE DUE			
6 '83			

WITHDRAWN

Deterring Criminals

Policy Making and the American Political Tradition

Jeffrey Leigh Sedgwick

CARL A. RUDISILL LIBRARY
LENOIR RHYNE COLLEGE

American Enterprise Institute for Public Policy Research
Washington, D.C.

Jeffrey Leigh Sedgwick is assistant professor of political science at the
University of Massachusetts.

364.973

Se 2d

114834

July 1980

Library of Congress Cataloging in Publication Data

Sedgwick, Jeffrey Leigh.
    Deterring criminals.

    (AEI studies ; 280)
    1. Criminal justice, Administration of—United
States.   2.   Crime and criminals—Economic aspects—
United States.   3.   Corrections—United States.
I.   Title.   II.   Series: American Enterprise
Institute for Public Policy Research.   AEI studies ;
280.
HV8138.S39   364'.973   80-13350
ISBN 0-8447-3385-7

© 1980 by the American Enterprise Institute for Public Policy Research,
Washington, D.C. All rights reserved. No part of this publication
may be used or reproduced in any manner whatsoever without permission
in writing from the American Enterprise Institute except in the case of
brief quotations embodied in news articles, critical articles, or reviews.
The views expressed in the publications of the American Enterprise Institute
are those of the authors and do not necessarily reflect the views of the
staff, advisory panels, officers, or trustees of AEI.

"American Enterprise Institute" and (AEI) are registered service marks of
the American Enterprise Institute for Public Policy Research.

Printed in the United States of America

CONTENTS

INTRODUCTION   1

1   CRIME, CONSUMER SOVEREIGNTY, AND THE   5
     AMERICAN REGIME

     Welfare Economics and Democracy   6
     American Political Thought   7

2   AN ECONOMIC THEORY OF CRIMINAL BEHAVIOR   16

     Economic Model of Crime   16
     Evidence on Deterrence   22
     Conclusion   25

3   ALLOCATING RESOURCES IN LAW ENFORCEMENT   27

4   REHABILITATION, DETERRENCE, AND   35
     RETRIBUTION

     Rehabilitation   36
     Deterrence   39
     Retribution   43
     Conclusion   46

5   CONCLUSIONS   48

INTRODUCTION

Americans are currently showing a renewed interest in the problem of law and order, which is hardly strange since crime has been an important and perennial political issue in the United States. Insofar as public order and safety are conditions for the pursuit of human happiness, crime is of fundamental concern to self-interested men.

One aspect of this concern over law enforcement is the extent to which it reflects a contest between two opposing approaches. The current debate is not so much over the relative importance or priority of the crime problem as it is over what to do with criminals so as to reduce the crime rate. On the one side are the advocates of rehabilitation; on the other, the advocates of deterrence. To a great degree, these two contesting factions are dominated by social scientists who use conflicting hypotheses of criminal motivation, each supported by its own type of research. The rehabilitation camp has long been dominated by sociologists and psychologists, while the deterrence camp is increasingly dominated by welfare economists.

This conflict raises an interesting question: Can social science lead to the adoption of public policies that are in the public interest? A successful effort would have two features. First, the particular approach used should result in the adoption of policies that achieve the desired result. For example, cost-benefit analysis in law enforcement is useful only insofar as it identifies programs that demonstrably lower the crime rate. Second, the approach chosen must produce policies consonant with the moral and constitutional requirements of the American regime if the policies are to be publicly defensible. In other words, policy research ultimately is judged by its ability to produce effective and constitutional solutions to public problems.

The purpose of this study is to investigate whether micro-

1

economics or welfare economics can generate effective and constitutional solutions to the problem of crime. Currently, economic models of deterrence and criminal motivation are gaining support. At the same time, there is a growing realization that attempts at rehabilitation have shown little success. The use of welfare economics in formulating policy is not free of problems, however; for, while such models probably should replace older causal theories of criminal motivation, their use may lead the policy maker into an excessive and unwise dependence on public preferences in formulating law enforcement goals.

That public opinion may occasionally diverge from the public interest is the central problem in the American political tradition. Perhaps Hamilton put it most clearly in *Federalist*, No. 71:

> It is a just observation that the people commonly *intend* the PUBLIC GOOD. This often applies to their very errors. But their good sense would despise the adulator who should pretend that they always *reason right* about the *means* of promoting it. They know from experience that they sometimes err; and the wonder is that they so seldom err as they do. . . . When occasions present themselves in which the interests of the people are at variance with their inclinations, it is the duty of the persons whom they have appointed to be the guardian of those interests to withstand the temporary delusion in order to give them time and opportunity for more cool and sedate reflection.[1]

The American political tradition may best be characterized as a delicate balance between the practice of democratic government and the preservation of fundamental values, such as the equal rights of all men. The Declaration of Independence sets the tone of American political life by focusing on this basic tension. It claims that men are endowed by their Creator with rights, among which are the rights to life, liberty, and the pursuit of happiness. Governments, in contrast, are instituted by the consent of the governed. Thus, political rule or authority has no such apparent basis as human rights do. In the absence of such a basis, governments are judged by the degree to which they respect and promote man's natural rights. Yet is it not apparent that throughout history consent has been given to governments or regimes that have *not* respected natural rights? Thus, that which is consented to may diverge from what nature or the Creator prescribes.

---

[1] Alexander Hamilton, James Madison, and John Jay, *The Federalist Papers*, Clinton Rossiter, ed. (New York: Mentor, 1961), p. 432.

Put simply, wisdom and consent exist together in our political tradition. Yet there is an irresolvable tension between the two; they cannot be reconciled in any simple way. The task of the policy maker defined by our political tradition is to bring them together. Total reliance on either wisdom or consent to the exclusion of the other would be improper. To the extent that welfare economics relies wholly on consumer sovereignty or public preference to identify desirable policies, that paradigm may be incompatible with American political tradition and the public interest.

1

Crime, Consumer Sovereignty, and the American Regime

This chapter will deal with the congruence between American political philosophy and the welfare-economics approach to crime. It is almost trite to say that we wish to formulate and implement policies that are in the public interest, but this emphasizes that policies must be judged by the standard the regime sets for itself.

The American Founding Fathers appealed to a set of principles defining what is good. From these, a system of government is derived; and from the operation of that system, policies are derived. The crucial question is whether the policies implemented accord with the principles of the regime. It would be an exhausting task to try to answer this question for each individual policy. A possible shortcut would be to use an analytic approach that is itself congruent with American political philosophy. If the conceptual framework selected to analyze a problem affects the type of policy ultimately recommended, then the adoption of an approach to policy compatible with American tradition should considerably increase the likelihood that specific policies emanating from that approach would accord with our political philosophy.

First of all, the fundamental statement of American political philosophy is the Declaration of Independence. It provides insight into how the Founding Fathers understood themselves and their actions in creating a new political order. One indication of the central role of this document is Lincoln's reference to it as an "apple of gold," with the Constitution but a "picture of silver, subsequently framed around it."[1] To judge whether welfare economics is consonant with American political thought, its underlying philosophy has to be

---

[1] Abraham Lincoln, *The Collected Works of Abraham Lincoln*, Roy P. Basler, ed., 9 vols. (New Brunswick: Rutgers University Press, 1953), vol. 4, p. 169.

compared with the philosophy of the Declaration of Independence. Such a comparison shows that welfare economics has a simplistic notion of democracy in that it recognizes only half of the American political tradition. The reliance of welfare economics on consumer sovereignty parallels the Declaration's argument that governments are based on the consent of the governed. In short, consumer sovereignty is analogous to popular sovereignty. However, welfare economics has no analogy to the Declaration's insistence on the natural rights of men, which makes its congruence with American political philosophy problematical. A fuller comparison of welfare economics and American political thought will support this tentative conclusion.

Welfare Economics and Democracy

James M. Buchanan has cogently argued that welfare economics is more democratic than majority voting in a simple democracy. A welfare-economics approach to formulating law enforcement policies would compare estimated benefits or public willingness to pay for the policy with estimated program costs. If benefits exceeded costs, the program would be implemented. In a simple voting democracy, a majority of voters would decide whether or not a program was implemented. If a minority of voters wanted a particular program initiated very badly, the intensity of their preference would presumably be reflected in a great willingness to pay for that program. If the total amount that this minority shows a willingness to pay were greater than the total program cost, then the program would be funded, despite the fact that it was supported by only a minority of citizens. Thus, as Buchanan points out, a market system allows a greater range of alternatives and can satisfy minority preferences better than simple majority voting.[2] A welfare-economics approach to public policies can actually protect minority rights by taking account of intensity of preferences in a manner that one-man, one-vote democracy cannot. Minority tastes are not made irrelevant simply because they belong to a minority.

A welfare-economics approach to selecting public policies seems highly democratic since policies are based on public preferences and their intensity. These advantages all stem from the central role of consumer sovereignty or public preferences in selecting policies. But

[2] James M. Buchanan, "Individual Choice in Voting and the Market," *Journal of Political Economy*, vol. 62, no. 4 (August 1954), p. 338.

consumer sovereignty is not without problems. What weight is to be given to ignorant or ill-advised preferences in policy making? Suppose the public is willing to pay the higher cost of walking patrolmen as opposed to patrolmen riding in cars because they imagine that walking patrolmen are more effective in fighting crime, despite research evidence to the contrary. What weight should be given to these mistaken preferences? Should more money be spent to put policemen on walking beats?

Even if consumer preferences are not ignorant or ill-advised, they may change frequently. I suspect that public willingness to pay for law enforcement programs rises after news reports of particularly horrifying crimes. After a short time, memory of the crime fades, and the level of support for increased police protection falls. The policy maker is now left with the difficult problem of which willingness to pay is the *true* preference. Since neither of the two expressed preferences is superior in theory to the other, is it desirable to try and shift resources as public preferences change? In view of the sometimes fickle nature of public opinion, it is possible that, by the time public preferences are measured and appropriate policies implemented, opinion may have changed so much that the implemented policies may no longer be optimal. Given the serious nature of law enforcement and its relation to the health of society, one wonders whether law enforcement should be wholly based on the shifting sands of public opinion.

The possibility of ignorant or ill-advised public preferences and of shifts in these preferences over time points up a fundamental question: do the American people have a stable, long-term interest in law enforcement that may diverge from their expressed opinions on the subject? If so, then the goal of policy analysis should be to articulate this interest and base public policy on it rather than on stated public preferences. In order to deal with such a possibility, I turn to an investigation of American political thought.

American Political Thought

The logical beginning for a study of American political thought is the Declaration of Independence. The fundamental feature of that document is the tension between government by consent of the governed and the preservation of natural rights. This tension is due not to the incompatibility of these two principles but rather to their interdependence. Popular sovereignty is justified by the equal rights of all men and the resulting need for each man to have a vote to defend his rights. The source of tension is the possibility that the exercise of popular sovereignty may result in the limitation or abridgment of some men's rights. Thus, a delicate balance must be preserved between the two principles.

The example of chattel slavery shows how a popular government could conceivably vote to abridge or totally deny the rights of a particular minority. The reader of the Declaration will notice that men are endowed with certain rights by their Creator, not by mutual consent. In this way, the Declaration is careful to set the question of rights apart from that of consent. If these rights with which man is endowed by his Creator represent a type of natural wisdom, then the Declaration reflects a potential tension between wisdom and consent.

Given this tension in the Declaration of Independence, the principal task of the Founding Fathers was to develop a form of government that could strike a balance between popular sovereignty and respect for human rights. That this task was recognized by the founders is clearly seen in the argument of *Federalist*, No. 10, whose second sentence notes that even friends of popular government are alarmed by the propensity of popular governments toward faction.[3] Factions are to be deplored not only for their propensity to introduce instability and confusion into public councils, but also because they lead to decisions being made "not according to the rules of justice and the rights of the minor party, but by the superior force of an interested and overbearing majority."[4]

Indeed, Madison (under the pseudonym of Publius) defines faction in such a way as to point out the necessity for conflict between faction and human rights: "By a faction I understand a number of citizens, whether amounting to a majority or minority of the whole, who are united and actuated by some common impulse of passion, or of interest, adverse to the rights of other citizens, or to the permanent and aggregate interests of the community."[5] Madison points out the potential conflict between wisdom and consent by arguing that, if a majority faction ever formed in a popular government, the rights of the minority would not be protected. Incidentally, the last line of the preceding quotation is revealing, for Madison suggests that a nation has permanent and aggregate interests distinct from the interests or passions of the majority or minority. Hence

---

[3] Alexander Hamilton, James Madison, and John Jay, *The Federalist Papers*, Clinton Rossiter, ed. (New York: Mentor, 1961), p. 77.

[4] Ibid.

[5] Ibid., p. 78.

Madison shows his readers that the opinions of the citizenry do not necessarily articulate the long-term or permanent interests of the community.

Given that factions are destructive of minority rights, the question becomes: How does one deal with faction in a popular government? Madison points out that there are two choices—either remove the cause of faction or control its effects. To remove the cause of faction, one would have either to destroy the liberty that permits faction to grow or to give to every man "the same opinions, the same passions, and the same interests."[6] The first remedy would resolve the tension between wisdom and consent by abolishing consent. Madison refers to this remedy as worse than the disease. The second remedy would require that all men become alike in their interests and opinions. Madison argues that this solution is wholly impractical, since the sources of faction are deeply embedded in the nature of man. For example, Madison suggests that human reason and self-love are connected: man uses his reason to protect and promote his own interest. As a result, opinions become intertwined with passions. The opinions of the mind are influenced by the passions of the body. The most obvious fact about mankind is that each of us has his own body; and consequently, our passions and self-love set us apart from one another. To give all men the same opinions or passions would require the destruction or overcoming of individual bodies.

Giving all men the same interests would prove just as difficult. Madison comments that men's different kinds of property holdings originate in different individual faculties. Again it would appear that the source of different interests lies in the fact of individual bodies. Insofar as men have individual and unique bodies, they will come to acquire various and unequal amounts of property. And, as Madison points out, "the most common and durable source of factions has been the verious [sic] and unequal distribution of property."[7] Short of abolishing liberty or destroying the individuality of man, it appears that faction cannot be avoided in politics.

If faction cannot be avoided, then its effects must be controlled. One cannot expect faction to be controlled and moderated by enlightened statesmen, for, as Madison reminds his readers, "enlightened statesmen will not always be at the helm."[8] Rather, Madison suggests two solutions, the principle of representation and the enlargement of

---

[6] Ibid.
[7] Ibid., p. 79.
[8] Ibid., p. 80.

the orbit of government. These two principles together constitute what he calls a republic. Representation consists of the people selecting a small number of men to operate the government in the name of all the people. The principal advantage of representation is "to refine and enlarge the public views by passing them through the medium of a chosen body of citizens, whose wisdom may best discern the true interest of their country and whose patriotism and love of justice will be least likely to sacrifice it to temporary or partial considerations."[9] One might well question why the people should recognize and elect men of good character rather than men willing simply to pander to faction. After all, Madison does point out that statesmen are not always available. Here the effect of enlarging the orbit of government is felt. In a large republic, particularly one based on commerce, the number of different interests is necessarily greater. Therefore, to be elected, a representative will be forced to appeal to different and potentially conflicting interests by finding a common ground. As long as there is no majority faction, moderation and compromise will be necessary. And when each individual faction is a minority of the whole, all factions have a common interest in protecting minority rights.

The central contention of Madison's argument is that public opinion or public preference is an uncertain basis for decent government. Public opinion is most likely to manifest itself in what he calls faction, and he is very careful to point out that faction is contrary to the permanent and aggregate interests of the community. Consequently, republican government is necessary if wisdom and consent are to be made compatible in American politics. Representation is necessary to "refine and enlarge" public opinion, while enlargement of the orbit of government is necessary to frustrate potentially majoritarian factions and to make moderation indispensable.

The potential conflict between wisdom and consent is a recurrent theme in American political thought. Abraham Lincoln considers this same question in his "Address Before the Young Men's Lyceum of Springfield, Illinois," delivered in 1838. This speech is particularly relevant here, since it considers crime and public responses to crime. Interestingly, the speech is entitled "The Perpetuation of Our Political Institutions."[10] Lincoln begins by arguing that the chief danger to American freedom is not external but internal. He comments that "if destruction be our lot, we must ourselves be its author and

---

[9] Ibid., p. 82.
[10] Lincoln, *Collected Works*, vol. 1, p. 108.

finisher. As a nation of freemen, we must live through all time, or die by suicide."[11] That suicide, Lincoln argues, would take the form of an increasing disregard for the law.

As early as 1838, Lincoln saw signs of that disregard for law. He introduces two specific examples, which he calls "the most dangerous in example, and revolting to humanity."[12] The first is the Mississippi case where a mob began hanging all the gamblers in town. Once the gamblers were all hanged, blacks were hanged on the pretext that they were planning an insurrection. Then whites suspected of sympathizing with blacks were hanged; and finally strangers were hanged. To make the horror of this spectacle more vivid, Lincoln comments: "Thus went on this process of hanging, from gamblers to negroes, from negroes to white citizens, and from these to strangers; till, dead men were seen literally dangling from the boughs of trees upon every road side; and in numbers almost sufficient to rival the native Spanish moss of the country, as a drapery of the forest."[13] The second case Lincoln introduces as a very short story which "is, perhaps, the most highly tragic, of any thing of its length, that has ever been witnessed in real life."[14] A mulatto man, living in St. Louis, was seized by a mob, dragged to the edge of town, chained to a tree, and burned to death. Lincoln carefully avoids mention of the reason for this individual's treatment. The audience is invited to feel outrage and disgust at the treatment of this man regardless of his crime.

Only after mentioning these two examples as horrible, dangerous, and tragic does Lincoln enlighten his audience with some interesting information. In the first case, Lincoln suggests that gamblers follow a useless and dishonest occupation. Of these two criticisms, I believe the first is the more telling, for Lincoln says that gamblers "constitute a portion of population, that is worse than useless in any community; and their death, if no pernicious example be set by it, is never matter of reasonable regret with any one. If they were annually swept, from the stage of existence, by the plague or small pox, honest men would, perhaps, be much profited, by the operation."[15] Lincoln's argument is that simple self-interest dictates that we not regret the hanging of gamblers because they are of no interest to us. But note the effect of following the logic of self-interest. An action originally designed

---

[11] Ibid., vol. 1, p. 109.
[12] Ibid.
[13] Ibid., vol. 1, p. 110.
[14] Ibid.
[15] Ibid.

only to strike at worthless gamblers eventually was extended to a class of people, strangers visiting Mississippi on business, who cannot be considered worthless in general. Once one class was judged useless without a trial, what prevented other classes of men from being so judged until bodies hung from the trees like Spanish moss? If we can agree that the latter situation is undesirable, then simple self-interest would appear to be insufficient in explaining law enforcement. The dictates of self-interest do not necessarily coincide with the right of all men to a fair trial.

If Lincoln's first example is designed to show the insufficiency of self-interest in explaining law enforcement, then his second case is designed to show the insufficiency of retribution. When Lincoln first discusses the burning of the mulatto in St. Louis, he ignores the question of the man's guilt. Later, Lincoln reveals that the mulatto "had forfeited his life, by the perpetration of an outrageous murder, upon one of the most worthy and respectable citizens of the city; and had he not died as he did, he must have died by the sentence of the law, in a very short time afterwards."[16] Why, then, is this example of revenge so tragic and horrifying? Had not the mob executed the man, the law surely would have. Why should legal justice be preferred to mob justice if the result is the same?

It is Lincoln's argument that the results of mob justice and legal justice are never the same. While it is true that the direct consequences of the two examples Lincoln mentions were good, the indirect consequences were serious enough to outweigh the direct consequences. The indirect consequences of mob justice are well illustrated in the Mississippi case. Once mob justice takes precedence over legal justice, matters quickly get out of hand. As Lincoln says, "When men take it in their heads to day, to hang gamblers, or burn murderers, they should recollect, that, in the confusion usually attending such transactions, they will be as likely to hang or burn some one, who is neither a gambler nor a murderer as one who is; and that, acting upon the example they set, the mob of to-morrow, may, and probably will, hang or burn some of them, by the very same mistake."[17]

The origin of this problem lies in the very character of the modern, Lockean regime. Whereas the ancient regime buttressed its laws with civic religion or a "noble lie," the modern regime's law is obviously a human contrivance. This conventional law stands in stark contrast to individual opinions about justice which are connected to

---

[16] Ibid.
[17] Ibid.

self-love. In the liberal regime, the individual comes to see his own opinions on justice as more valid than the obviously compromised dictates of the law. Liberal or liberated man forgoes the middling sort of legal justice the regime offers in favor of the pursuit of absolute justice, as defined by his conscience. But one would do well to remember Madison's observation that reason, interest, and passion are so influenced by self-love that they become contrary to just and decent government. Lincoln's two examples reinforce this same point. Modern man needs to pay attention to the forms of legal justice rather than to listen only to his interests, his passions, or even his own conscience.

Once mob justice replaces legal justice, lawlessness spreads rapidly. As Lincoln comments, the example of unpunished mob justice encourages the lawless in spirit to become lawless in practice.[18] As lawlessness spreads, even the good people in the regime become disenchanted with the laws and come to favor any change in the form of government, since they imagine that they have nothing to lose. At this point, Lincoln perceptively notes, "men of sufficient talent and ambition will not be wanting to seize the opportunity, strike the blow, and overturn that fair fabric, which for the last half century, has been the fondest hope, of the lovers of freedom, throughout the world."[19] It is in this manner that the indirect consequences of mob justice lead to the destruction of the American regime.

Up to this point in the Lyceum Speech, Lincoln demonstrates the possible destructive effects of interest and retribution on political freedoms. In the rest of the speech he makes suggestions for remedying these defects. It is important to recognize the order of Lincoln's argument. He begins by suggesting the inculcation of a political religion that would dictate absolute adherence to the law. Consider the rhetoric of this argument:

> Let every American, every lover of liberty, every well wisher to his posterity, swear by the blood of the Revolution, never to violate in the least particular, the laws of the country; and never to tolerate their violation by others. . . . Let reverence for the laws, be breathed by every American mother, to the lisping babe, that prattles on her lap . . . in short, let it become the *political religion* of the nation; and let the old and the young, the rich and the poor, the grave and the gay, of all sexes and tongues, and colors and conditions, sacrifice unceasingly upon its altars.[20]

---

[18] Ibid., vol. 1, p. 111.

[19] Ibid., vol. 1, pp. 111–112.

[20] Ibid., vol. 1, p. 112.

Can it be doubted that the teaching of such an uncalculating reverence for the law is meant to offset the tendency of liberated men to view everything, including obedience to the law, in self-interested terms? Lincoln goes so far as to suggest that even bad laws should be religiously observed until they are legally repealed lest the example of civil disobedience once again unleash the lawless in society.[21]

Following his suggestion for a political religion, Lincoln turns to the question of ambition. Ambition is nothing more than a type of self-interested behavior. But it can threaten the American regime. Lincoln suggests that ambitious men may no longer be satisfied to serve the country as they once had. During the early years of the regime, this country was a noble experiment in self-government, and those who aided in the success of that experiment could expect to share in the glory of success. But once the experiment proved successful, glory could no longer be acquired by serving the regime. Men of ambition may therefore seek glory not in serving this regime, but in founding new regimes. About this type of man Lincoln comments: "Distinction will be his paramount object; and although he would as willingly, perhaps more so, acquire it by doing good as harm; yet, that opportunity being past, and nothing left to be done in the way of building up, he would set boldly to the task of pulling down."[22] What will stand in the way of such ambitious men?

When the memories of the Revolution were fresher in men's minds, the pride of the people and their hatred of the British combined to support the new country. But those memories faded with time. Lincoln argues that sober reason has to take the place of these forgotten and faded memories. Reasoned reflection on ambition shows men that they have an interest in obeying the law if only to frustrate the ambitious who would tear down the fabric of their liberty. Thus, interest can be made to counteract ambition by supporting obedience to law.

Yet Lincoln's argument does not stop with reasoned self-interest; his essay ends with the exhortation that "those materials be moulded into *general intelligence, sound morality* and, in particular, *a reverence for the constitution and laws*; and, that we improved to the last; that we remained free to the last; that we revered his name to the last; that, during his long sleep, we permitted no hostile foot to pass over or desecrate his resting place; shall be that which to learn the last

---

[21] Ibid.

[22] Ibid., vol. 1, p. 114.

trump shall awaken our WASHINGTON."[23] Clearly this ending is an appeal to whatever patriotism was left in Lincoln's audience. His solution to the problem of perpetuating our political institutions thus has three parts: political religion, reasoned self-interest, and patriotism.

The fundamental point of Lincoln's Lyceum Speech is the necessity of adhering to the law rather than obeying one's own conscience about justice. The fact that law in a Lockean state is obviously conventional and contractual makes obedience to the law tenuous. Obedience can come in one of three ways. It can be stimulated by self-interest when the law is seen as a means of securing freedom and property. Since self-interested men want to acquire property, obedience to the law becomes a matter of fundamental interest to each man in a Lockean state. This is the middle part of Lincoln's argument. But self-interest is not sufficient to secure obedience to the law, for it can lead to mob justice or attempts to overthrow the government. Consequently, Lincoln suggests that obedience to the law be supported by political religion and patriotism, neither of which is based on calculations of self-interest. But their prominence in the Lyceum Speech indicates their crucial role in maintaining American freedom. Lincoln's speech points to the ultimate insufficiency of self-interest alone in maintaining the regime.

In summary, the American regime is based on the tension between wisdom (which proclaims the rights of all men) and consent, or the practice of popular sovereignty. The recurrent theme of both *The Federalist* and Lincoln's Lyceum Speech is the necessary but problematic character of self-interest in maintaining political freedom. Self-interested opinions must be enlarged and refined through representation and modified by political religion and patriotism if wisdom is to be protected.

---

[23] Ibid., vol. 1, p. 115.

2

An Economic Theory
of Criminal Behavior

In this chapter I will investigate the economic approach to the problem
of crime. The economist believes that the choice of criminal behavior
reflects an individual's desire to maximize his utility subject to various
constraints on his opportunities. The economist's goal is to propose
a theory of behavior that will enable him to understand crime. Beyond
that, the theory must make it possible to predict how various government programs affect crime rates. The object is to formulate public
policies that will both deter people from choosing crime and be compatible with American legal and moral traditions. Achieving this end
requires an appropriate approach to policy and an enlightened understanding of its advantages and shortcomings.

Economic Model of Crime

The economic model of criminal behavior has a fundamentally different perspective from that of the differential-association model often
attributed to sociologists. These sociologists tend to see criminals as
essentially different from law-abiding people because of the different
associations the criminals have had since birth. Economists suppose
that, however much criminals and law-abiders differ in their motivation, they both respond similarly to changes in the opportunity sets
that they confront. Consider Isaac Ehrlich's comments:

> Much of the search in the criminological literature for a
> theory explaining participation in illegitimate activities seems
> to have been guided by the predisposition that since crime is
> a deviant behavior, its causes must be sought in deviant
> factors and circumstances determining behavior. Criminal
> behavior has traditionally been linked to the offender's

presumed unique motivation which, in turn, has been traced to his presumed unique inner structure, to the impact of exceptional social or family circumstances, or to both. . . . [The economist's] alternative point of reference, although not necessarily incompatible, is that even if those who violate certain laws differ systematically in various respects from those who abide by the same laws, the former, like the latter, do respond to incentives.[1]

Ehrlich goes on to argue that it is useful to analyze crime not only in terms of unique personal motivations and attributes but also in terms of incentives that affect criminal and law-abider alike.[2]

The economic approach to crime thus offers the advantage of simplicity. Rather than two distinct theories to explain human behavior, one for deviants and one for nondeviants, one theory of utility maximization is sufficient to explain and investigate both types of behavior. Surely, if two explanations of human behavior are equally valid, the more universally applicable should be preferred.

Discovering what incentives lead individuals to commit crimes requires a model of utility maximization subject to constraints. Gary Becker has formulated a model that focuses on the constraints facing the potential criminal.[3] In this model, the volume of offenses committed by a person is determined by the probability of his conviction per offense, his punishment per offense, and a portmanteau variable representing all other variables influencing the volume of offenses. If criminals react to the costs of committing crimes, then the first derivatives of the volume-of-crime function with respect to probabilities of conviction or severity of punishment should be negative. That is, as the probability of conviction or the severity of punishment increases, the amount of crime should decrease, other things being equal.

Becker's model is a good beginning. Its advantage is its central focus on two variables affecting the crime rate that can easily be manipulated by the government. However, the portmanteau variable hides a wealth of influences on the crime rate. For example, part of the costs of crime are its opportunity costs, the legal opportunities that the individual forgoes to pursue crime. The rate of unemployment

<hr>

[1] Isaac Ehrlich, "Participation in Illegitimate Activities: A Theoretical and Empirical Investigation," *Journal of Political Economy*, vol. 81, no. 3 (May/June 1973), pp. 521–522.

[2] Ibid., p. 522.

[3] Gary S. Becker, "Crime and Punishment: An Economic Approach," *Journal of Political Economy*, vol. 76, no. 2 (March/April 1968), pp. 169–217.

in society is at least somewhat manipulable by the government and influences the opportunity cost of crime. Furthermore, a life of crime and a life of legal activity need not be mutually exclusive. An individual could mix legal and illegal activities in various proportions. Thus, a more comprehensive model of human behavior should be developed that reflects variables such as unemployment, legal earning opportunities, and the benefits of successful criminal activity.

Ehrlich has suggested a model with the desired features.[4] His model begins with the simple hypothesis that one's utility in a particular state of the world is a function of one's wealth or "stock of a composite market good" and the amount of time devoted to consumption as opposed to earning or accumulation. The individual allocating his time among consumption, legal activity, and illegal activity has two potential futures: either he will be arrested and punished or whatever crimes he commits will go undetected. The initial presumption about man was that he is a utility-maximizer. Thus, to determine whether a man will become a criminal, the relative amounts of time devoted to consumption, crime, and legal enterprise must be varied until the unique distribution is found that yields the highest expected utility net of costs. Ehrlich argues that, given an amount of time allocated to consumption, the optimal allocation of labor between legal and criminal activity must satisfy the condition that the ratio of incomes produced by time spent in legal and illegal activity must equal the ratio of utilities associated with income derived from legal and illegal activity (unless all working time is spent in one activity or the other).

This model has many interesting implications. First, in order to prevent specialization in illegal activity, it is necessary "that the potential marginal penalty . . . exceed the differential marginal return from illegitimate activity . . . , for otherwise the marginal opportunities in [illegal activity] . . . would always dominate those in [legal activity]. . . ."[5] If, for example, the penalty associated with a specific criminal act were not greater than the net gain from the act, then, regardless of the probability of conviction, crime would always pay. Ehrlich's conclusion is that concurrent penalties should be discontinued. The practice of sentencing criminals to concurrent prison terms means that there is a positive marginal punishment for the first offense but none for all subsequent offenses. Consequently, if

---

[4] Ehrlich, "Participation in Illegitimate Activities," pp. 521–565.

[5] Ibid., pp. 526–527.

the criminal has any reason to expect concurrent sentences if convicted, he has a positive incentive to commit multiple offenses.

A second important implication has to do with the stigma society attaches to the ex-convict. The economic model shows that the choice of legal or illegal activity depends on the relative costs and benefits in the legal and illegal markets. If these costs and benefits remain the same, then criminals will tend to repeat their crimes, while noncriminals will tend to obey the law. In fact, however, the relative cost and benefits tend not to remain the same for convicted criminals. The stigma attached to the ex-convict decreases his legal earning opportunities relative to continued crime and hence may necessitate his continuing to commit crimes. Perhaps one way to correct this situation would be to adopt penalties that seem proportionate to the crime so that when the convict is released from prison he will appear, in the eyes of the public, to have "paid for his crime." This should make it easier to lift the stigma from him.

An alternative solution to the crime-inducing incentive of criminal stigmatization has been suggested by Daniel Glaser. He correctly points out that labeling can encourage recidivism through decreasing legitimate opportunities for the released offender. He then observes that "to publicize a person's delinquent or criminal record may produce only a greater probability of crime repetition. Usually the record need be known by only a few officials. Accordingly, an important aspect of planning for crime reduction is to provide for the security and restricted access of criminal record information."[6] This conclusion neglects the deterrent value of criminal stigmatization. If a prospective criminal realizes that society will brand him as an undesirable if he commits crimes, then the expected costs of crime are higher than they would otherwise be. In effect, the threat of losing status deters crime. But Glaser's suggested policy would remove that deterrent and thereby require a new deterrent, such as more certain or more severe punishment, if the crime rate is not to rise. All other things held equal, keeping criminal records secret may reduce the labeling that leads to recidivism, but it will also lower the costs of committing a crime. The issue, then, is to balance a credible deterrent against the destructive labeling that closes off legal work opportunities.

An important factor of the criminal-behavior model not yet discussed is the individual's attitude toward risk. The risk-preferrer gains positive utility from taking a risk. The risk-neutral person

---

[6] U.S. National Institute of Mental Health, *Strategic Criminal Justice Planning* (Washington, D.C., 1975), p. 84.

neither likes nor dislikes risk, while the risk-avoider dislikes bearing risk. Hence, not all individuals view a choice in the same manner. A deterrent sufficient to make a risk-neutral person indifferent in choosing between legal and illegal activities would not be sufficient to deter a risk-preferrer but would be more than sufficient to deter a risk-avoider. As Ehrlich points out,

> Whether offenders are likely to specialize in illegitimate activity thus becomes an aspect of their attitudes toward risk, as well as their relative opportunities in alternative legitimate and illegitimate activities. Also, whether in equilibrium, crime pays or does not pay in terms of expected (real) marginal returns is simply a derivative of an offender's attitude toward risk, since in equilibrium the expected marginal returns from crime would exceed, be equal to, or fall short of the marginal returns from legitimate activity depending on whether the offender is a risk avoider, risk neutral, or risk preferrer, respectively.[7]

Although the government can do little to change the risk preferences of its citizens, it is important to remember that the combination of punishment and probability of conviction necessary to deter crime will be influenced by the specific risk preference of each individual criminal.

An interesting implication of risk preference for the economic model of crime has to do with the presumption of an upward-sloping crime-generation function for society. (Such an upward-sloping function implies that the volume of crime increases as the benefits of crime increase, ceteris paribus.) Depending on risk preference, some people will choose to commit crime although expecting a very low (or negative) net benefit. More risk-averse persons will move into the criminal sector only if they expect higher net benefits. Therefore, even if each individual in society made an all-or-nothing choice between crime and legal activity according to his assessment of the prospects, society as a whole would exhibit an upward-sloping supply curve of crime. The reason is that as the net benefits of crime rise, a greater number of risk-averse individuals would enter the illegal sector, thereby increasing the volume of crime.

At this point, the objection may be raised that the economic model of criminal behavior describes wealth-generating crimes, such as larceny and burglary, but fails to describe the so-called "crimes of passion." This objection, however, arises from a misunderstanding of

---

[7] Ehrlich, "Participation in Illegitimate Activities," p. 528.

the economist's position, which is not simply that man is a wealth-maximizer. The economic model can be applied to any situation where an individual is seeking to maximize his subjective utility. Thus, the fact that crimes of passion often do not involve transfers of money does not mean that they cannot be explained by the economic model.

An economist would explain murder as one example of the broader situation in which an individual's utility or well-being is intertwined with the utility of another. The actions of one person directly affect the welfare of another. (Incidentally, this interdependence does not work through the price system. Economics teaches that all actions are interrelated. Most actions can be coordinated through the prices for goods and services prevailing in the market-place. But, in the case of interdependent utilities, the interdependences work directly, outside the market system.) Presumably the murderer or rapist gains utility or satisfaction from inflicting harm on his victims. That is, the murderer or rapist enjoys the discomfort of others. Consequently, the murderer would be willing to expend effort to make others worse off as long as the utility gained from the discomfort of others exceeds the disutility of the effort required to create that discomfort.

While it is unlikely that society can prevent some people from enjoying the misfortune of others, society can raise the cost of inflicting discomfort in a number of ways. Potential victims can be warned of the dangers and urged to take reasonable precautions; the law can be enforced more strictly; prison terms can be lengthened and made mandatory. The point to be stressed in discussing crimes of passion is that the economic model can explain even seemingly unplanned and unpremediated crimes. But how well does this model predict reality? A provisional answer follows in the next section, but note should be taken here of Ehrlich's findings.

> The rate of specific felonies is found to be positively related to estimates of relative gains and negatively related to estimates of costs associated with criminal activity. . . . Moreover, the elasticities associated with crimes against the person are not found to be lower, on the average, than those associated with crimes against property.[8]

If Ehrlich's studies can be repeated and verified, then perhaps the presumption should be discarded that all crimes against persons are unplanned "crimes of passion" that cannot be deterred.

---

[8] Ibid., p. 560.

Evidence on Deterrence

The economic model of criminal behavior assumes that such behavior can be understood as a variant of the theory of occupational choice. That is, criminals become criminals because crime offers greater net benefits than any available legal opportunity. The implication of this argument is that the crime rate can be lowered either by raising the expected costs of crime or by making legal opportunities more attractive. If criminals rationally choose to commit crimes, then they can be deterred by manipulating the costs and benefits of crime. This section will review some of the growing evidence from current research that crime can be deterred.

The government could conceivably decrease the relative attractiveness of crime in two ways. First, it might seek to make legal opportunities more attractive by increasing the number and the wages of jobs available in legal enterprise. Second, it could seek to increase the cost of committing a crime. The anticipated costs of crime depend on the interaction of two separate variables—the certainty of arrest and the severity of punishment. The law enforcement system in the United States could readily affect both of these variables in order to raise or lower the relative attractiveness of crime and hence the crime rate.

While earlier studies are not unanimous on the effect that manipulation of certainty and severity of punishment has on the crime rate, most recent studies do not reject the deterrence hypothesis. A brief categorization of these studies follows.

Perhaps the most frequent approach to testing the deterrence hypothesis is the correlation of national data on crime rates with length of imprisonment and indicators of certainty of punishment. Generally, data derived from the Uniform Crime Reports and the National Prisoner Survey are broken down by state and used in a comparative analysis. Most of these analyses show a statistically significant inverse relation between index crime rates and certainty of punishment.[9] There is less agreement that severity of punishment and index crime rates are negatively related, even though some studies have found such a correlation.

Perhaps the best-known deterrence study using aggregate national data is Ehrlich's, completed in 1973. In the first section of this chapter, Ehrlich's model of criminal behavior was reviewed. Ehrlich

---

[9] The seven FBI index crimes are nonnegligent homicide, rape, assault, robbery, burglary, larceny in excess of $50, and auto theft.

also empirically tests his model, using state-by-state index crime data and National Prisoner Survey data for 1940, 1950, and 1960. Then he tries to construct a proxy for the estimated gains from crime.

> We postulate that payoffs on such [property] crimes depend, primarily, on the level of transferrable assets in the community, that is, on opportunities provided by potential victims of crime, and to a much lesser extent on the offender's education and legitimate training. The relative variation in the average potential illegal payoff, Y_i, may be approximated by the relative variation in, say, the median value of transferrable goods and assets or family income across states which we denote W. The preceding postulate also implies that those in a state with legitimate returns well below the median have greater differential returns from property crimes and, hence, a greater incentive to participate in such crimes, relative to those with income well above the median.[10]

By this process, Ehrlich hopes to construct a crude measure of the net benefit of illegal compared with legal opportunities. The median value of assets and goods in a state gives some indication of the potential benefits of property crime. Then the percentage of families with legal earning opportunities less than the mean of all families below the state median was computed. It would be expected that, as the median value of assets increases, ceteris paribus, the gains from property crime would increase and so would the property crime rate. Likewise, as the percentage of families below one-half of the median income in the state increases, ceteris paribus, the rate of property crime would be expected to increase since the disparity between legal and illegal wages would increase.

In evaluating his data, Ehrlich finds three specific results. First, for all seven of the FBI index crimes, crime rates vary inversely with measures of the certainty and severity of punishment.[11] Second, crimes against property (including robbery, burglary, larceny, and auto theft) vary positively with median income and percentage of families below one-half of the median personal income in the state. However, these two variables are not as strongly related to rates of personal crime.[12] Third, "all specific crime rates appear to be positively related to the percentage of nonwhites in the population."[13] In summary,

[10] Ehrlich, "Participation in Illegitimate Activities," pp. 538–539.

[11] Ibid., p. 545.

[12] Ibid.

[13] Ibid.

23

Ehrlich concludes that his results are not inconsistent with the deterrence hypothesis.

Ehrlich's study provides support for both the economic model of criminal behavior and the deterrence hypothesis. His major innovation was roughly to approximate the gains from property crime and then use that estimate to discover that property crime rates vary positively with the potential gains from crime. This indicates that criminals may pursue a wealth- or utility-maximizing strategy. Ehrlich's most stunning discovery, though, is that rates of crimes against the person, so-called crimes of passion, respond just as strongly to expected costs of punishment as do property crimes, which are traditionally thought to be calculated attempts to gain.[14]

The second main approach used in studying deterrence is the policy experiment: attempts are made to assess the deterrent effect of changes in law enforcement policies by comparing "before and after" data. Reported crime rates from before and after implementation of the new policies are analyzed for evidence of deterrence. An example of this type of policy experiment is Robert Chauncey's study of skyjacking.[15]

Chauncey studies the trends in skyjacking to determine whether it is possible to deter skyjackers. First, he plots the skyjacking rate as a function of time. Second, he notes certain "critical points" when the costs of skyjacking were raised through increased certainty or severity of punishment. Fortunately, in the case of skyjacking it is very easy to distinguish between policies affecting certainty (such as reciprocal treaties to return skyjackers to the country from which the plane was skyjacked and the installation of electronic monitoring devices at all airports) and policies affecting severity (increased penalties). By examining the skyjacking rate for two periods immediately before each critical point and two periods after, Chauncey hopes to be able to determine if there is any significant change in skyjacking rates attributable to the policy change. Also, the general trend of skyjacking rates over several years is used to check the critical points and make sure that changes apparently due to new policies were not, in fact, normal seasonal variations.

Chauncey selects five critical points—two involving certainty of punishment, two involving severity of punishment, and one involving a combination of both. His results indicate that increases in certainty

---

[14] Ibid., p. 560.

[15] Robert Chauncey, "Deterrence: Certainty, Severity, and Skyjacking," *Criminology*, vol. 12, no. 4 (February 1975), pp. 447–473.

of punishment yielded significant reductions in the skyjacking rate. Increases in severity of punishment produced no clear results, and neither did the certainty-severity combination.[16]

The third major approach to studying the deterrence hypothesis uses questionnaires to probe criminal behavior and individual perceptions of the certainty or severity of punishment. For example, Gordon Waldo and Theodore Chiricos attempt to study the effect of certainty and severity of punishment on crime rates by interviewing a group of 321 Florida State University students. They find no consistent relation between perceived severe punishment and self-reported crime, but they do find that perceived certainty of punishment is inversely related to admitted criminality.[17] In yet another study using the questionnaire approach, Irving Piliavin finds from a survey of male high-school students that expected costs of criminal behavior do have an inverse relation with self-reported crime rates.[18]

Conclusion

This brief survey of deterrence research is meant to give the reader a feeling for the types of research being done in law enforcement. But the key question for policy makers is whether this research provides support for the economic model of criminal behavior, and the answer is ambiguous. In a study commissioned by the National Academy of Sciences, Daniel Nagin reviews three reasons why most deterrence studies do not provide wholly compelling evidence. First, studies based on reported crime rates are not entirely dependable, owing to variations over time and across police jurisdictions in reporting crimes to the FBI. Second, there is a two-way relation between sanctions and crime rates. So far, no one has devised an entirely satisfactory way of statistically separating the effect of crime rates on sanction levels from the effect of sanction levels on crime rates. As a result, estimates of the effect of sanctions on crime rates are not totally reliable. And, finally, Nagin suggests that "the inverse association between crime

---

[16] Ibid., p. 467.

[17] Gordon P. Waldo and Theodore G. Chiricos, "Perceived Penal Sanction and Self-Reported Criminality: A Neglected Approach to Deterrence Research," *Social Problems*, vol. 19, no. 4 (Spring 1972), p. 536.

[18] Irving M. Piliavin, Arlene C. Vadum, and Jane Allyn Hardyck, "Delinquency, Personal Costs and Parental Treatment: A Test of a Reward-Cost Model of Juvenile Criminality," *Journal of Criminal Law, Criminology and Police Science*, vol. 60, no. 2 (June 1969), p. 168.

and sanctions also reflects, at least in part, incapacitation effects [of imprisonment] rather than deterrent effects."[19]

What, then, should be made of these studies and the economic model of crime? Should they be ignored if they cannot be wholly trusted? I suggest not. Rather, since we must act on less than perfect knowledge, it seems reasonable to accept the verdict of the National Academy's Panel on Research on Deterrent and Incapacitative Effects that "the evidence certainly favors a proposition supporting deterrence more than it favors one asserting that deterrence is absent."[20] And, to the extent that deterrence appears to work, it supports the economic model of criminal behavior.

---

[19] National Academy of Sciences, Panel on Research on Deterrent and Incapacitative Effects, *Deterrence and Incapacitation: Estimating the Effects of Criminal Sanctions on Crime Rates*, Alfred Blumstein, Jacqueline Cohen, and Daniel Nagin, eds. (Washington, D.C., 1978), p. 98.

[20] Ibid., p. 47.

3

Allocating Resources
in Law Enforcement

The preceding chapter suggested that criminals respond to incentives just like other people. By manipulating the costs and benefits of crime, society can raise or lower the crime rate. The next step in formulating a rational policy for law enforcement would be to establish what level of law enforcement is appropriate for society. Some may argue that the only appropriate level is one that eradicates crime. But while that may be technically possible, the costs of such a policy would most likely be exorbitant, especially in view of the multitude of other demands on public funds. Without an endless supply of public funds and with more demands on public coffers than funds to satisfy those demands, the public is faced with the economic problems of choice and scarcity. It seems logical that public funds should be spent where the need is greatest, but the question is how to determine the priority of public needs and the appropriate level of public funding.

Perhaps the first question should be why there is a public demand for law-enforcement policies, why there should be a *public* policy. Welfare economists stress the ability of the private market, in most cases, to provide goods to the public at the lowest possible cost, thereby satisfying the greatest quantity of public wants with a given amount of resources. The government bureaucracy cannot hope, through authoritative allocations, to match the subtle coordination of the price system prevailing in the free market. But where the market fails to obtain an efficient solution because of unpriced external effects of private actions or where public goods are to be provided, the government often needs to act.

The demand for public policies against crime is an indication that the private market has failed to provide sufficient law enforcement. We might agree that life without public law enforcement (or, as

Hobbes called it, the state of nature) is "solitary, poor, nasty, brutish and short"[1] since, in such a situation, each individual rationally waits for his neighbor to accept the burden of enforcing the law and providing security. He hopes to obtain, free, the benefits of living in a protected neighborhood. Also, where each man provides or purchases his own law enforcement, he selects which laws he wishes to enforce. The result is a multitude of legal systems. When these systems come into conflict in the absence of a common superior arbiter, the result is anarchy where might makes right. The individual with the strongest law enforcement agency necessarily prevails in such a state.

The nonoptimal level of law enforcement prevailing in the state of nature means that life is necessarily insecure and unfree. Therefore, men agree upon the need for public or common policies against crime. The problem then becomes how public officials determine the appropriate amount of law enforcement to provide. This problem would be easily solved if the public could produce, package, and market discrete units of law enforcement to citizens who did not engage in strategic behavior. However, this approach is impossible because law enforcement is a public good and the benefits provided to one member of society "spill over" to his neighbors. Thus, the amount of law enforcement freely purchased in a "public-goods market" is too small. Each man waits for his neighbor to buy.

Therefore, one amount of law enforcement must be selected for the whole neighborhood. The criterion used by economists in identifying this socially optimal level of law enforcement is Pareto optimality. A particular policy is said to be Pareto optimal "if it is impossible to make some consumer better off without simultaneously making others worse off."[2] By this definition, very few policies may appear to be Pareto optimal, since for almost any change of policy there will be gainers and losers. However, if the gainers from a particular policy could fully compensate the losers and still be better off themselves, then the policy would be a potential Pareto improvement on the status quo.[3] A Pareto optimum is a policy on which no further Pareto improvements can be made.

Welfare economists argue that public policies should be funded if

[1] Thomas Hobbes, *Leviathan*, Michael Oakeshott, ed. (New York: Collier-Macmillan, 1962), p. 100.

[2] Richard G. Lipsey and Peter O. Steiner, *Economics*, 3rd ed. (New York: Harper and Row, 1972), p. 293.

[3] E. J. Mishan, *Cost-Benefit Analysis: An Informal Introduction* (London: George Allen & Unwin, 1975), p. 390.

the cost of the program is less than the benefit, as measured by the public's willingness to pay for it. The cost of providing a commodity is that commodity's opportunity cost, which, in turn, represents the next best alternative use of the inputs required to produce the good in question. Therefore, where the benefit-cost ratio of a particular program exceeds unity, one can infer that the public estimates the benefit of that program to exceed the benefit of the required inputs in their best alternative use. Hence, inputs should be bid away from their less preferred uses and combined in their more preferred use. Where the benefit-cost ratio of a program is unity, one can infer that the public is indifferent in choosing between the utility of those inputs in the proposed program and the utility of the same inputs in their next best alternative use. A benefit-cost ratio of less than one means that the benefits of the proposed program are less than the potential benefits of the program's inputs when shifted to their best alternative use.

The above logic suggests that when all new public programs (and all additions to, or subtractions from, existing programs) are evaluated on a benefit-cost basis, then the resulting distribution of public inputs yields the maximum net social benefit. No other redistribution of inputs, goods, or services can yield a higher utility. Thus, the condition resulting from the application of the benefit-cost ratio is an optimum in terms of total social utility.

Let us put aside for a moment the marginal cost of crime prevention or law enforcement and try to understand how to measure the benefits of law enforcement. The first proposition is that the costs of crime determine the benefits of law enforcement. This proposition can easily be proved by the following argument. According to economic theory, if an individual is subject to a certain type of cost or disutility, he should be willing to pay any amount less than the dollar value of that disutility to be rid of it. For example, if a particular person causes me great uneasiness, which I value at $100, and if that person could be persuaded to move to another neighborhood for $80, then I could obtain a net benefit of $20. In fact, I would be better off if I could bribe my neighbor to move for any amount less than $100. Thus, the cost my neighbor imposes on me places an upper limit on the amount I would be willing to pay to see him move away.

An individual's willingness to pay for a good or service is a way of representing his demand for that good or service. Demand reflects the benefit that the consumer expects to receive from the good in question. Thus, the costs of crime can be said to determine an individual's demand, or willingness to pay, for law enforcement, which reveals the benefit of law enforcement. Clearly, the costs of crime avoided by a particular law enforcement program measure the benefits of the program.

A moment's thought yields an intuitive idea of the shape of the demand function for law enforcement. The marginal cost of successive crimes is likely to increase since criminals become bolder with practice and success and will attack more secure or better guarded targets. As a consequence, society will bear increasing psychic costs in fear. With the increasing marginal costs of crime (both monetary and psychic), the first few units of crime prevention are likely to yield very high benefits. Where crime rates, and thus fear of crime, are high, the utility of law enforcement is very high. However, for successive units of law enforcement, the benefits and therefore public willingness to pay will decline. The more increments of law enforcement provided, the lower the crime rate drops. The lower the crime rate, the lower are the psychic costs of each individual crime prevented, and thus the lower is the public willingness to pay for that unit of crime prevention. Also, as more law enforcement is provided, the quality of criminal targets will decline. The bigger targets will be protected first, so only relatively marginal criminal opportunities will remain. Thus, the demand curve for law enforcement is most probably downward sloping to the right, reflecting diminishing marginal benefits of law enforcement. At some point, the marginal benefit per dollar of further expenditures on law enforcement will fall below the marginal benefit per dollar of other alternative uses of public funds. This reflects the fact that, as the crime rate falls, other public problems begin to appear relatively more pressing.

The policy maker begins his analysis of the optimal level of law enforcement by specifying in detail all the public programs contributing to crime reduction. Then the effectiveness of each separate program has to be determined. This is done by determining what percentage decrease in the crime rate is achieved by each unit of the program. At this point the public decision maker has the data necessary for determining the cost-effectiveness of each program, which tell administrators the number of crimes prevented by a dollar spent in each of a multitude of law enforcement programs. Law enforcement officials will then presumably select the most cost-effective program as a means of fighting crime.

But the analysis is not yet completed. Just because a particular policy has the highest cost-effectiveness ratio of all possible law enforcement programs does not mean that it should automatically be adopted. Rather, the decision maker must find out if the public wants to spend its money on law enforcement or education, health maintenance, or national defense. It is conceivable that the public might be willing to put up with current crime rates and wish to spend public dollars in some other area.

Therefore, the administrator must combine cost-effectiveness data with data on the public's demand for, or willingness to pay for, crime prevention. Suppose that the public were willing to pay more to prevent a specified amount of crime than it would cost. In that case, the decision maker should increase the amount of work in the most cost-effective program by one unit. Now the entire process is repeated. As argued earlier, the public is likely to exhibit decreasing willingness to pay for successive units of crime prevention since, as crime rates decline, other public problems will appear more serious relative to crime. Thus, the public will be less willing to spend its tax dollars on crime prevention and more willing to fund other public goods.

On the other hand, for any one law enforcement program, the costs per unit of crime reduction are likely to increase for added increments of activity, barring any technological change, because, as law enforcement is intensified, the less clever criminals are taken out of circulation. This means that it becomes increasingly hard to deter or incapacitate the remaining active criminals and, therefore, costs per unit of crime reduction rise. Also, for the first few increments of law enforcement, inputs are bid away from lower-valued alternative uses. The opportunity cost of the program in question rises as these inputs are bid away from progressively more valuable alternative uses.

If consumer willingness to pay declines and per unit costs of crime reduction increase as program size increases, then a point will be reached where public demand exactly equals the cost of provision of the public good or service in question. At this point of equality between marginal cost and marginal benefit, the program has reached its optimal size.

Given this criterion of the optimal level of crime, some of the ways in which economists apply it should be examined. In his 1968 article, Gary Becker suggests that social loss from crime be defined as a function of the amount of damage from crime plus the cost of law enforcement.[4] Society would then be served by minimizing the amount of social loss from crime, using the choice variables available to decision makers.

The idea of a social loss function and its relation to the optimality

[4] Gary S. Becker, "Crime and Punishment: An Economic Approach," *Journal of Political Economy*, vol. 76, no. 2 (March/April 1968), pp. 169–217.

criterion just discussed needs to be explained. It was said that law enforcement programs should be expanded until the marginal social benefit equaled the marginal social cost. For all units of law enforcement up to that point, it was tacitly assumed that the marginal benefit of crime prevention exceeded the marginal cost. It should be remembered that the benefit of a unit of crime prevention equals the physical and psychic damage from crimes that are averted by the law enforcement. Therefore, the statement that a unit of law enforcement should be provided if it adds more to benefits than to costs can be interpreted to mean that the costs of suffering the avoidable crimes are greater than the costs of preventing those crimes. This conclusion bridges the gap between the Pareto optimality criterion and the minimization-of-social-loss criterion in analyzing crime policy. The Pareto criterion suggests that, where crime prevention is cheaper than suffering the crime, society should replace the costs of experiencing the crime by the costs of preventing the crime. At some point, however, possible further increments of law enforcement will be more costly than bearing the costs of crimes directly. At that point, society's costs are minimized by accepting the costs of crime and forgoing further units of law enforcement.

If the policy maker is to minimize social loss, he must begin by identifying the components of social loss from crime. The first such component is the physical and psychic loss from crime itself. Crime imposes two kinds of costs on the public: one is direct, such as lives lost, dollars stolen, property destroyed; and the other is the psychic cost of fear. These damages are a function of the number of offenses; the total amount of damage from crime to society is likely to increase with the number of offenses.

There are other components of society's loss from crime. A major one is the cost of apprehension and conviction, which is a function of the amount of law enforcement, itself, in turn, a function of the amount of inputs such as capital, labor, and resources. The presumption is that more inputs mean more arrests and more convictions. But more convictions mean higher costs, *ceteris paribus*, although an advance in law enforcement technology could eventually lead to lower costs for more activity.

The costs of apprehending and convicting criminals do not include the costs of punishment. Obviously it costs a great deal of money to operate state and federal prison systems. Thus the policy maker would want to consider the cost to society of punishing criminals. For each type of punishment, there is a specific cost. For example, if a criminal is sentenced to prison, the per capita cost of running a prison for a year times the length of the prison sentence measures some of the social costs of punishment. If the sentence takes the form of a fine, then the social cost of punishment consists of the collection costs only. This calculation can be made for all other forms of punishment also.

The total social loss from crime, thus, is composed of three costs: the cost of apprehension and conviction, the harm done to citizens by crime, and the cost of inflicting punishment.

Some readers may be troubled by the analysis presented up to this point. If the goal of crime policy is to minimize social loss from crime, then it would be logical for the policy maker to switch to less expensive and more severe punishments as an inexpensive means of deterring crime. As George Stigler has pointed out, very severe punishments are sometimes cheaper than less severe punishments. For example, executing criminals is cheaper than supporting prison systems for long terms, and seizing all a criminal's assets is only marginally more expensive than levying a small fine.[5] Becker's analysis, however, does not inevitably lead to this result, for the social cost of punishment used in his calculation of social loss reflects society's distaste for a punishment deemed far too severe for the crime committed. Consequently, it is unlikely that Becker's model would lead to the widespread use of very severe punishments, since that would actually raise society's costs of dealing with crime.

A slightly different method of calculating social loss from crime might also lessen the danger that overly severe punishments will be resorted to in order to increase deterrence. Becker's formulation focuses on manipulation of certainty and severity of punishment as a means of influencing the rate of offenses in society. John R. Harris has suggested that Becker "derives criteria for optimal levels of expenditure on law enforcement and form of punishment subject to a given legal framework. The point of this paper is that the legal framework need not be taken as constant but is itself subject to policy choice."[6] Harris's point is that certain institutional changes could be made that would lower the costs of arresting and convicting criminals, the certainty and severity of punishment being fixed. However, these same institutional changes could also increase the probability of wrongfully convicting and punishing an innocent person. It would be less costly, for example, to convict a given percentage of arrested

[5] George Stigler, "The Optimum Enforcement of the Laws," *Journal of Political Economy*, vol. 78, no. 3 (May/June 1970), p. 527.

[6] John R. Harris, "On the Economics of Law and Order," *Journal of Political Economy*, vol. 78, no. 1 (January/February 1970), p. 165.

suspects if the rules governing admissibility of evidence in a court-room were relaxed. Yet, if they were relaxed, the probability of convicting an innocent person would increase.

Put in formal terms, one could say that, "as the probability of a guilty person going unpunished (a Type I error) is reduced the probability of an innocent person being punished (a Type II error) is increased. The lower the cost of apprehending and punishing a given proportion of offenders at a given level of offenses, the higher will be the incidence of wrongful punishment."[7] Thus, an addition could be made to Becker's social-loss function to represent the social loss from wrongful punishment of innocent people, which, according to Harris, would be a function of the probability of an offender's being arrested and convicted, the number of offenses, the degree of legal safeguards for suspects, and the punishment meted out upon conviction. The implication of this addition is to raise the optimal level of crime in society above that specified in Becker's model since, as Harris points out, "the optimal intensity of apprehension and the level of punishment will likely be lowered when social costs of unjust convictions are taken into account."[8]

This chapter has presented a technique for determining the optimal level of law enforcement in society that entails identifying the physical and psychic harm inflicted by crime, the costs of apprehension and conviction, the costs of wrongful conviction and punishment, and the social cost of punishing criminals. The most important attribute of this technique is that it bases law enforcement on subjective perceptions of the costs of crime and hence willingness to pay for law enforcement. Public resources are shifted among different policies in accordance with public preferences. The explicit goal is to maximize social welfare or utility, but social welfare is understood simply as the summation of private interests or utilities. As suggested in the first chapter, such reliance on public preference may be unwise. It appears at the very least to reflect only a partial understanding of the intent of the Founding Fathers.

One might well wonder whether such a partial understanding is necessarily a bad thing. After all, the founders themselves may have misunderstood the character of democracy. In the next chapter, I will argue that the economists' simplistic reliance on public preference is not only unwise but also self-defeating, since law enforcement cannot succeed where obedience to law is understood in purely self-interested terms.

---

[7] Ibid., p. 166.

[8] Ibid., p. 169.

4

Rehabilitation, Deterrence, and Retribution

Up to this point, I have attempted to analyze the economic approach to criminal behavior and law enforcement. Empirical research increasingly supports the economic model of criminal behavior, and the economic approach to law enforcement planning helps to rationalize and coordinate the multitude of public programs in this area. The welfare-economics approach to crime, however, is not free of all problems, one of which is its treatment of punishment. The economic approach to punishment tends to emphasize deterrence to the extent of forgetting other possible aspects of punishment.

In discussing punishment, three different approaches should be considered. The first, which can be labeled rehabilitation, considers only the needs of the criminal. Treatment of the criminal and his restoration to mental health becomes of paramount concern; punishment seems a poor word for this endeavor. The second approach, which can be labeled deterrence, asks what punishment is necessary to prevent the commission of the crime and thus focuses on man's criminal tendencies. Third is retribution, which focuses not just on the criminal or man's criminal tendencies but rather on the specific criminal act. Retribution demands that punishment be made to fit the crime; it asks "an eye for an eye, and a tooth for a tooth."

Ultimately, punishment must be accounted for according to these three approaches. In this chapter, I shall argue that the economists' single-minded concern with punishment as deterrence is self-defeating and will result in an inability to punish any individual criminal and hence an explosive growth in crime rates. To support this contention, I shall briefly investigate each approach to punishment.

Rehabilitation

Rehabilitation as an approach to punishment carries great weight in contemporary society, largely because of its espousal by the dominant school of criminology, sociological criminology. Those who follow this approach view the criminal with some degree of sympathy. After all, he did not choose to commit crimes; he is a product of his environment, none of which he himself can be held responsible for. From this perspective, the purpose of punishment is not to inflict pain or to deter others but to treat the criminal, to restore him to "law-abiding health." But proponents of rehabilitation must answer two very difficult questions: First, does rehabilitation work? Second, regardless of whether it works, is it desirable?

There are two ways of investigating the effectiveness of rehabilitation. First, one can look at the logic of rehabilitation. If, as Edwin Sutherland and Donald Cressey argue, an individual's receptivity to group behavior patterns is determined by earlier group associations and so on back to birth,[1] then it seems highly unlikely that a criminal will accept the law-abiding values and habits of his treatment or therapy group. Rather, he will "play the game" to win his release and then return to his old patterns of behavior. Another theoretical defect in the rehabilitation literature is the tendency to overlook the effect of rehabilitation on deterrence. Often, attempts to rehabilitate convicted offenders make punishment less uncomfortable. To the extent that punishment loses its discomfort, it becomes less severe and less capable of deterring potential offenders. However, many advocates of rehabilitation neglect this trade-off. This is understandable since the rehabilitation approach presupposes causality or determinism of criminal behavior, while deterrence is based on the presumption of choice by the potential criminal. The mounting evidence for deterrence reviewed in Chapter 2 raises the questions about the theory justifying rehabilitation.

But what is the empirical evidence? Does rehabilitation work? The academic and scientific journals have been filled with a lively debate over just this question for the past several years. Perhaps the focus of the debate has been Robert Martinson's study of the effectiveness of various types of rehabilitation programs, including educational and vocational training programs for young offenders, adult training programs, individual counseling, group counseling, transforming the

---

[1] Edwin H. Sutherland and Donald R. Cressey, *Criminology*, 8th ed. (Philadelphia: J. B. Lippincott, 1970), p. 85.

institutional environment, changing sentencing strategies, releasing convicts, and so on.[2] Martinson reviews all the methodologically sound studies on rehabilitation published in English between 1945 and 1967 and reaches the conclusion that, in these 231 studies, *"the rehabilitative efforts that have been reported so far have had no appreciable effect on recidivism."*[3] By this Martinson means that, although some programs were apparently effective, the successful programs were so few and far between that no pattern emerged indicating the efficacy of a particular type of treatment for specific types of offenders.

One reason for the lack of evidence supporting rehabilitation is the apparent inability of corrections officials and social scientists to correctly predict violent behavior in inmates. Success in rehabilitating offenders depends, at least in part, on an ability to correctly identify the social pathologies that influence criminal behavior. Knowledge of these pathologies would make it possible to predict—with a high degree of accuracy—that offenders with those characteristics would commit violent crimes in the future. Empirical studies show that such predictive abilities are currently poor.

For example, the National Acadamy of Sciences reviewed a number of studies that attempted to predict violent acts of recidivism. One typical study is that of Cocozza and Steadman, who identify 257 indicted felony defendants found incompetent to stand trial in New York State in 1971 and 1972 and then narrow the group down to 160 defendants eventually released either to the community or to mental institutions. These 160 defendants were classified as dangerous or nondangerous by two psychiatrists; the follow-up period for the study was three years. Table 1 gives the relevant statistics. The reader should note that only slightly more than half the violent offenders were correctly identified in advance. For each violent offender correctly identified, six nonviolent offenders were misclassified as violent. On the whole, for every two offenders correctly classified, three were incorrectly classified.

Despite this evidence of the inability to correctly identify and treat potential repeat offenders, some will argue that more money is needed for further research on rehabilitation. They will argue that insufficient attempts have been made to rehabilitate, atlhough the 231 studies reviewed by Martinson seem to counter this argument. But

---

[2] Robert Martinson, "What Works?—Questions and Answers About Prison Reform," *The Public Interest*, no. 35 (Spring 1974), pp. 22-54.

[3] Ibid., p. 25.

TABLE 1
Prediction of Violent Acts of Recidivism

	Percentage	Number
Offenders	100	160
Predicted dangerous	60	96
True positives	14	13
False positives	86	83
Predicted nondangerous	40	64
True negatives	84	54
False negatives	16	10
Recidivism rate	14.8	
Correctly classified offenders	42	
Incorrectly classified offenders	58	
Correctly classified violent offenders	56.6	

SOURCE: National Academy of Sciences Panel on Research on Deterrent and Incapacitative Effects, *Deterrence and Incapacitation: Estimating the Effects of Criminal Sanctions on Crime Rates*, Alfred Blumstein, Jacqueline Cohen, and Daniel Nagin, eds. (Washington, D.C., 1978), p. 249.

there is no need to refute this argument. Rather, the question remains whether successful rehabilitation is desirable. Rehabilitation presumes that some defect in the offender leads him to commit crimes and that treating it will prevent recidivism. It might seem, according to this view, that the sentence served by the offender should be determined by the probability of recidivism. But would such sentencing accord with public preference? That is, would the public be satisfied if longer sentences of confinement and treatment were given to prostitutes than to murderers? After all, prostitutes repeat their offenses much more frequently than murderers. In fact, the typical murderer never repeats his crime. Therefore, he needs no treatment and should be set free.

I suspect that there would be a great public outcry if judges began issuing sentences based purely on a rehabilitation philosophy, which shows that the public understands punishment as something other than simple rehabilitation. One possible explanation is self-interest. People want to see murderers sentenced to longer terms than prostitutes because murderers harm innocent people while prostitutes engage in "victimless" crimes. But might not that missing element also be retribution? Might not the public want to see the murderer sentenced more severely than the prostitute precisely because the crime of murder is more serious than the crime of prostitution? Regardless of whether the public desire for punishment is based on self-interest or retribution, it seems highly undesirable to view punishment simply as rehabilitation; the American people would most likely be outraged if murderers were let off and prostitutes and alcoholics confined.

Deterrence

The deterrent view of punishment considers not the crime nor the criminal but rather all other men. That is, the severity of one man's sentence depends on the propensity of other men to commit a similar crime. But is it right to use one man as a means of teaching others?

Putting aside this difficult question, one might wonder if a single-minded concern with deterrence is sufficient cause for punishment. To James M. Buchanan, deterrence alone is problematical justification for punishment. He develops his argument under the rubric of the "punishment dilemma," which begins with the point that a society will be characterized by laws that are good because they impose order and stability on what would otherwise be chaotic anarchy. That is, individual citizens will find it in their interest to create laws in order to structure social existence.[4] But, while law and civil society are more in the interest of man than the state of nature, it is even more in the interest of any individual man to break the law and take advantage of others who obey it. Consequently, self-interested men will not consistently obey the law in the absence of some enforcement mechanism.

Buchanan suggests that, according to the economic approach to crime, men could be prevented from committing crimes by the threat of punishment. But law enforcement is costly both in identifying criminals and imposing actual punishments. Buchanan divides the costs of punishment into two parts: first, the monetary costs of prisons, guards, security systems, et cetera; and second, the psychic costs. He argues that

> the basic costs of punishment are subjective, and these can best be conceived in a utility dimension. The imposition of penalties on living beings, whether or not these beings have

[4] James M. Buchanan, *The Limits of Liberty: Between Anarchy and Leviathan* (Chicago: The University of Chicago Press, 1975), p. 130.

violated law, causes pain, utility loss, to the normal person who must, directly or indirectly, choose these penalties. "Punishing others" is a "bad" in economic terms, an activity that is, in itself, undesirable, an activity that normal persons will escape if possible or, failing this, will pay to reduce.[5]

This distaste for, or disutility from, punishing stems from two sources, according to Buchanan. The first is an individual's fear that he himself may be the object of similar treatment in the future. Many people probably feel that they have done something criminal in their lives and that it is only by chance that they escaped arrest while others did not. The second is the possibility of punishing an innocent man. Together, these two reasons explain why there are psychic as well as monetary costs of punishment.

The "punishment dilemma" derives "from the elementary fact that to secure the public good of law-abiding the public bad of punishment must be accepted."[6] The dilemma is minimized if penalties are chosen before the commission of a crime because then they can be determined by equating the marginal cost of increments of punishment with the marginal benefits of increased law-abidingness. But after a crime is committed there is an almost irresistible impulse to abandon ex ante decisions in favor of reactive punishment decisions.

For, once a crime has been committed, the benefits of punishment appear in a different light. Punishment, or the threat of it, did not deter the particular criminal. Further, the marginal effect of punishing this criminal on all other potential criminals is very small. Consequently, the benefits of punishment appear smaller in the particular case than they appear before the crime had been committed. On the other hand, it is quite likely that the costs of punishment appear larger after the crime than during a rational, ex ante discussion of costs and benefits of law enforcement. It is one thing to concede philosophically the utility of capital punishment and quite another to sentence an actual human being to death. If both the marginal costs and the marginal benefits of law enforcement appear different after the crime is committed, then actual willingness to punish will very probably diverge from a declared willingness to punish criminals.

If the benefits of punishment appear to diminish after a crime is committed and if the costs appear to rise, men will obviously find it in their interest to impose less punishment in a particular case than they agreed ex ante. As a consequence, the deterrent effect of

---

[5] Ibid., p. 133.

[6] Ibid., p. 133.

threatened punishment diminishes and more crimes are committed. As more crimes are committed, the sentence in each individual case has less effect on total deterrence. Hence, the marginal deterrent benefit of each particular sentence decreases and even less punishment is administered. The result is an unstable situation where increasingly more crimes are committed and increasingly less punishment imposed until society returns to anarchy.[7]

Buchanan's description of the punishment dilemma puts the problem of deterrence in a new light. The usual fear of most critics of deterrence has been the use of cheap but excessively severe penalties. For example, Franklin Zimring and Gordon Hawkins argue that "it is not deterrence as an objective that is cause for concern but the escalation of sanctions for deterrent purposes. Thus, the moral problems raised by punishment for deterrent purposes arise only when we impose a punishment for deterrent purposes that is more severe than would otherwise be imposed."[8] From Buchanan's argument, the fear of excessive punishment can be seen to be unfounded. The real problem is that punishment will not be actually imposed. Statutory penalties may become more and more severe, but actual sentences meted out will be minimal as long as men consider only deterrence.

The crucial characteristic of the deterrence approach is that it considers only the effect of punishment on others in society. Utterly lacking here, as in the rehabilitation approach, is a concern for the intrinsic character of the crime committed. Buchanan claims punishment to be a psychic cost or disutility for men; that is, men have sympathy for the suffering of the offender. But why is this? How can men subtract the cost of the offender's suffering from the benefits of law enforcement? It is precisely because Buchanan, with his interest in deterrence, focuses only on the effect of punishment on others and weighs that benefit against the suffering of the offender. Never does Buchanan consider the possibility that men might look at the crime with anger or righteous indignation. The failure to analyze the intrinsic quality of the criminal act makes it possible to balance sympathy for the criminal against concern for deterring others.

Buchanan suggests that deterrence alone will result in a failure to punish and a return to anarchy. Walter Berns has suggested a similar outcome. He observes that "the modern purpose of punishment is not to teach men that it is immoral to commit a crime, even the crime of

[7] Ibid., p. 135.

[8] Franklin E. Zimring and Gordon J. Hawkins, *Deterrence: The Legal Threat in Crime Control* (Chicago: The University of Chicago Press, 1975), p. 39.

murder, but that it is contrary to their interests to do so."[9] Let us consider this point. If it were simply in men's interest to do what the law commands, self-interested men would need no law enforcement to watch over them; they would automatically obey the law. But it is clear that, in many cases, it is in one's interest to break the law if one can avoid detection. Consequently, men need law enforcement. The deterrence approach proposes that punishment be used simply to make illegal behavior unrewarding. But Buchanan's punishment dilemma shows that sufficient punishment will not, in fact, be meted out. Clever men will soon realize that, even if they fail to escape detection in evading the law, the punishment they receive will be insufficient to offset their gains from crime. Thus, crime will be rewarding, and it will increase in frequency.

Suppose society attempts to respond to the rising crime rates by increasing the severity of punishment. The attempt will fail because more severe punishments impose greater psychic costs on jurors and judges. Again, this is true as long as decision makers focus only on deterrence. Even increasing the certainty of arrest will be insufficient to reverse the rising tide of crime, since more arrests simply mean a lower marginal addition to deterrence from sentencing in each particular case. Berns concludes that, as long as men look upon crime simply as contrary to their interests and not as intrinsically wrong, the result will be that "the easily frightened will not break the law, but the fearless will break the law, . . . and the clever ones among them will do so with impunity."[10] Berns's argument is that, if calculating men see crime simply as contrary to their interests, they will constantly be watching out for opportunities when law enforcement is absent and crime pays. Buchanan's punishment dilemma suggests that the law enforcement system will constantly lack the resolve to impose punishment. As a result, crime will pay and men will commit crimes. If the major portion of a community is committing crimes, some with stealth and some brazenly, can it be doubted that the mutual trust and confidence of the citizenry will soon be undermined and the security that characterizes civil society will collapse? Men will return to the state of nature.

It appears, then, that deterrence alone is insufficient justification for punishment. The deficiency of that approach is a "softness" or lack of resolve to do what is necessary to prevent crime. The fact that

---

[9] Walter Berns, *For Capital Punishment: Crime and Morality of the Death Penalty* (New York: Basic Books, 1979), p. 138.
[10] Ibid., p. 139.

contemporary society has not yet returned to a state of nature (though some inner-city residents might disagree) reflects some other element in understanding punishment that permits judges and juries to hand down sentences, albeit with increasing hesitation. I propose that this other element, of which at least vestiges remain in our criminal justice system, is retribution.

Retribution

Retribution demands that punishment fit the crime. It is the desire for retribution that makes us punish murderers more severely than prostitutes, even though prostitutes are much more likely to repeat their offenses. And it is the need for retribution that provides us psychic satisfaction rather than pain in seeing a criminal get his just deserts. Yet no single concept is so deeply and fundamentally rejected in modern penology and criminology as retribution. Daniel Glaser argues that retribution is an artifact of older legal orders where politically dominant groups forced the weak to conform to established practices.[11] And Karl Menninger has suggested that the actual reason for punishment is nothing "but an irrational zeal for inflicting pain upon one who has inflicted pain (or harm or loss)."[12] But it is my contention that the desire for retribution (that is, righteous indignation) is a characteristic of any healthy legal system. Without a sense of retribution, there would be no respect for law, no ability to impose punishment, and no civil society.

First of all, a sense of retribution—or the desire to punish according to the severity of the offense—is necessary if punishment is actually to be imposed and criminals thereby deterred. As was argued earlier, deterrence without retribution results in an unwillingness to impose the statutory penalty for offenses. The consequence of this softness of public resolve is an ever-widening disrespect for the legal system and a growing crime rate. But what is the nature and origin of the impulse toward retribution? I suggest that it used to be known as righteous indignation, which term is preferable because it points at the origin of the impulse. Righteous indignation stems from a sense of right and wrong, for it is based on the intrinsic wrongness of the criminal act itself. Retribution and deterrence come from different

[11] U.S. National Institute of Mental Health, *Strategic Criminal Justice Planning* (Washington, D.C., 1975), p. 21.

[12] Karl Menninger, *The Crime of Punishment* (New York: Viking Press, 1968), p. 113.

sources, the former growing out of a sense of right and the latter out of a sense of self-interest, as Buchanan's discussion clearly shows.

The punishment dilemma shows that no legal system can survive as long as it is understood simply in terms of self-interest. This, in turn, implies that no civil society built upon a structure of law or legal order can survive if it is understood simply in terms of self-interest. If deterrence requires retribution, then self-interest requires a sense of right. But where does this sense of right come from? I submit that it is, at least in part, *created* by the law, for the law serves two distinct functions: it deters the criminal by the threat of punishment, and it teaches the law-abiding the difference between right and wrong.

Franklin Zimring has argued that the threat of punishment reduces crime in four ways: first, it is an aid to moral education; second, it is a habit-building mechanism; third, it builds respect for the law; and fourth, it gives a rationale for obedience to the law by making obedience more rewarding than crime.[13] Zimring notes that punishment makes individuals associate crime with bad consequences, which association gradually becomes transformed into the view that crime is wrong. A good analogy is the way in which parental punishment of a child's misbehavior becomes transformed in the child's mind into the idea that misbehavior is wrong. This process is what sociologists call internalization of norms or socialization. In the process of socialization, the consideration of crime shifts from whether it is profitable to whether it is right, and the difference is crucial. As long as a person considers crime simply from a self-interested perspective, he will commit crimes if he thinks that he can escape detection. However, once a person believes crime is decisively wrong, he is much less likely to commit an offense even if he knows that he could avoid detection. To enforce the law, the first person would have to be constantly watched; the second could be trusted.

When many different laws are combined, the individual habits of conformity become fused into a unified perception of right and wrong. Accompanying this view is a general respect for the law as the articulator of what is good or proper. It is from this moral sense that a desire for retribution or righteous indignation stems. The law-abiding individual will inevitably feel outrage at the sight of crime, which outrage is a product of the conflicting demands of right and self-interest. The law-abiding person obeys the law, even though he knows that it might occasionally be in his interest to break it and take advantage of

---

[13] U.S. National Institute of Mental Health, *Perspectives on Deterrence* (Washington, D.C., 1971), p. 4.

those who obey it. He forgoes this interest because he feels it right to obey the law. When he sees crime, he must either feel outrage at the unjust advantage taken by the criminal or else view himself as too timid to aggressively pursue his own advantage in a like manner.

It is precisely at this moment of hesitation between outrage and self-disgust that the public response to crime is decisive. As Zimring says, "If the solemn commands of a legal system were not reinforced with the threat of punishment, many individuals would see no basis for concluding that the legal system really meant what it said. More important, even those who would continue to obey legal commands would be demoralized by watching other people break the law and escape unpunished."[14] Lack of punishment thus diminishes deterrence for the calculating and makes the law-abiding doubt their own sense of right. The latter consequently will become more inclined to do what is in their interest as opposed to what is right. At the same time, the basis of the public resolve to punish, the impulse to retribution is weakened. Thus, less punishment will be meted out and the process is repeated. There can be little doubt that the crime rate will grow explosively and society will begin to disintegrate.

This connection of morality, law-abidingness, and the threat of punishment is supported by Matthew Silberman, who investigated why the threat of punishment has a different deterrent value for different people. In order to answer this question, he looks at the effect of a number of variables on the crime rate, including moral commitment, certainty of punishment, and peer involvement. He finds that moral commitment explains most of the variance, with peer involvement second. Of the three, certainty of punishment was the least influential determinant of crime rates.[15] These findings suggest that most people who do not commit crimes fail to do so because of a moral commitment to obeying the law. They see crime as wrong, not simply disadvantageous. This alone suggests the possibility of an explosive growth in crime if retribution were to be eliminated from law enforcement.

Silberman's study also sheds light on the possible source of moral commitment. He comments that

the pattern of correlations suggests that the apparent deterrent effect of the threat of punishment can be explained by the degree of moral commitment associated with a given

[14] Ibid., p. 5.
[15] Matthew Silberman, "Toward a Theory of Criminal Deterrence," *American Sociological Review*, vol. 41, no. 3 (June 1976), pp. 449–461.

offense. In other words, moral commitment to a given legal norm appears to be the mechanism by which the threat of punishment effectively constrains those who otherwise might be inclined to violate the norm. It seems that the threat of punishment produces lower crime rates because the threat of punishment increases the level of moral commitment to the legal norm which, in turn, reduces the incidence of crime.[16]

The threat of punishment does seem to build moral commitment and thereby deter crime. This evidence coincides nicely with the argument of Buchanan's punishment dilemma and Berns's suggestion that crime must be understood as wrong—not simply contrary to one's interest —if it is to be prevented. To the extent that modern penologists overlook retribution by focusing either on rehabilitation or on deterrence, they overlook a crucial factor in social control of crime.

In summary, it appears that a legal system that allows no room for retribution or righteous indignation is impotent. Such a system will lack the resolve or "hardness" necessary to punish criminals. Calculating men will, therefore, find it in their interest to commit more crimes. Confronted with frequent unpunished crimes, righteous men will conclude that their opinions about right and wrong are unsupported. This demoralization will result in the replacement of righteous indignation by envy of the successful criminal. Soon, self-interest will replace the sense of right, and men will commit even more crimes. Clearly, society needs the impulse to retribution in order to punish criminals. Equally clearly, the righteous need to witness punishment in order to maintain their belief in the rightness of what the law commands.

Conclusion

First of all, persons desiring deterrence of criminals should not overlook the importance of retribution. Without it, two things will happen. First, society will tend to see punishment as costly and will therefore fail to impose the level of punishment that was determined to be optimal before a particular crime occurred. The reason for this is the change in the way that the costs and benefits of punishment are perceived before and after the commission of a crime. After a crime is committed, the suffering of the criminal and the marginal effect of his particular punishment on the overall level of deterrence appear dif-

---

[16] Ibid., p. 451.

ferent from before the crime. Consequently, the public resolve to punish will weaken, and there will be a suboptimal level of punishment.

Second, if a sense of retribution is not encouraged and cultivated through just punishment of the guilty, then the law-abiding lose their sense of right and wrong and come to see the criminal-justice system as having no connection with right and wrong. They then ask themselves not whether breaking the law is wrong, but whether it is in their interest. As Silberman's research shows, moral commitment to a law is a much more effective deterrent than the belief that law-abiding behavior is in one's interest because of the certainty of punishment. Thus, the practice of punishing criminals reflects a merging of the deterrent and retribution approaches.

Punishment deters the interested by altering their calculation of the benefits and costs of crime. Punishment also creates a sense of moral commitment in citizens and sustains that sense by satisfying the righteous indignation of the law-abiding. Were the indignation of the law-abiding not satisfied through punishment of the guilty, the law-abiding would drift away from moral commitment and come to see the world simply in terms of self-interest. As Berns points out, this would mean the destruction of trust and security by the widespread growth of criminal behavior. Therefore, no law enforcement system and no government of law can exist without an effective punishment strategy grounded in both deterrence and retribution.

5

Conclusions

In the preceding chapter, I argued that self-interest is an insufficient basis for understanding punishment. Inferentially, then, welfare economics is insufficient for understanding punishment. If punishment is to be meted out, a sense of retribution is necessary in addition to deterrence. This sense of retribution is based on the intrinsic rightness or wrongness of the criminal act itself. The concern for deterrence, in contrast, is grounded in self-interest. In the first chapter, I argued that the American political tradition recognizes the importance of self-interest, but it also recognizes the ultimate inadequacy of self-interest in protecting human freedoms. It is precisely this latter argument that is lacking in welfare economics, with its emphasis on deterrence and self-interest.

At this point, it is clear that the welfare-economics approach to law enforcement, if allowed to override all other considerations, is incompatible with the American political tradition. Welfare economics suggests that the amount of resources devoted to law enforcement should be determined by citizen preferences. But if politics is the imperfect marriage of wisdom and consent, then it is possible that wisdom and consent may diverge. Citizens may fail to recognize and support good laws. That refusal may take the form of refusing to provide the resources to enforce the law. The economist's calculations would then dictate less law enforcement and more crime.

The evidence presented in the last chapter suggesting that law creates a moral consensus in society should be stressed. Law, in effect, teaches community values. The forms of justice refine the impulse to retribution and shape public perceptions of self-interest. If communities do not spontaneously coalesce and sustain themselves, then law must sometimes create and shape public preferences rather than simply reflect them. In this sense, the economist's approach wrongly assumes that the moral values of a community can be determined through consent. This is the implication of basing law enforcement, which creates and shapes moral values, on expressed public preferences. For example, would it be either wise or desirable to ask Americans if they are willing to pay for the enforcement of civil-rights legislation? Are not such laws promulgated precisely to change public preferences or opinions on race relations? If so, basing enforcement of these laws on public preferences would be irrational and self-defeating.

It seems reasonable to suggest that the welfare-economics approach to law enforcement is incompatible with the American system because it overlooks the possible conflict between wisdom (in the form of good laws) and consent (in the form of public willingness to pay for law enforcement). By ignoring the formative effect of law on public character, the economist reduces the problem of law enforcement to a consideration of what the public will pay for. But good laws are good regardless of public willingness to see them enforced. The highest goal of politics and policy making is to conjoin good policy with public willingness to support that policy. This goal cannot be attained by simply equating good policy with public preferences. Both must enter into the policy maker's consideration.

What are the implications of this argument for the type of man needed in policy making? What type of judgment is required to distinguish good from bad policy? It is my claim that welfare economics neglects the aspect of political leadership clearly implied by Madison's discussion of public preferences and faction in relation to decent government. Sometimes factions must be opposed, moderated, or enlightened. Popular government is good, but popular (or consumer) sovereignty should not rule independently of limits set by the recognition of a natural wisdom or good.

Raising the importance of wisdom in policy analysis brings up the two fundamental qualities of the responsible public official. First, he must be a man who understands the objectives of the regime, that is, a wise man. And, second, he must be a man of moral virtue or courage. The intelligence or wisdom to know the right objectives is necessary but not sufficient in a democracy. What, besides courage, can lead a public official to advocate a wise policy in the face of hostile public opinion and thus to serve the ends of the regime? The ability to use leadership rightly requires a moral quality or courage that is missing both from blind obedience to public preferences and from welfare-economics analysis.

In conclusion, welfare economics is a useful approach to law enforcement insofar as it leads the policy maker to ponder the best policy and insofar as the identification of that policy can be separated from occasionally ignorant or ill-advised preferences. The fact that ideal policy must be conceptually distinct from consent is derived from an understanding of one goal of the American regime—the preservation of human rights. Clearly men may consent to bad laws or fail to consent to good laws, and so consent cannot be the final word in policy making. But neither can welfare economics, for it fails to supply the moral or intellectual basis for leadership in policy making. Indeed, rather than recognizing the need to conjoin consent and wise policy, welfare economics wholly embraces consent. The policy maker is not encouraged to stand up for wise policy, but is reassured that he is serving the public's preferences. If the policy maker cannot wholly rely on welfare economics or consent, then he is dependent on his own devices to find the necessary skill and prudence in governing. Thus, just as the hammer cannot teach the apprentice carpentry, welfare economics cannot teach the policy maker how to govern.